Life Lessons

from THE INSPIRED WORD of GOD

BOOK of MARK

MAX LUCADO

General Editor

Scripture passages taken from:

The Holy Bible, *New Century Version*
Copyright ©1987, 1988, 1991 by Word Publishing. All rights reserved.

The Holy Bible, *New King James Version*
Copyright © 1979, 1980, 1982 by Thomas Nelson. All rights reserved.

All excerpts used by permission.

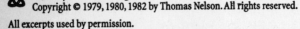

Design and cover art—by Koechel Peterson and Associates, Inc., Minneapolis, Minnesota.

Produced with the assistance of the Livingstone Corporation.

ISBN: 08499-5299-9
Published by Word Publishing

TABLE OF CONTENTS

HOW TO STUDY THE BIBLE

BY MAX LUCADO

*T*his is a peculiar book you are holding. Words crafted in another language. Deeds done in a distant era. Events recorded in a far-off land. Counsel offered to a foreign people. This is a peculiar book.

It's surprising that anyone reads it. It's too old. Some of its writings date back five thousand years. It's too bizarre. The book speaks of incredible floods, fires, earthquakes, and people with supernatural abilities. It's too radical. The Bible calls for undying devotion to a carpenter who called himself God's Son.

Logic says this book shouldn't survive. Too old, too bizarre, too radical.

The Bible has been banned, burned, scoffed, and ridiculed. Scholars have mocked it as foolish. Kings have branded it as illegal. A thousand times over it the grave has been dug and the dirge has begun, but somehow the Bible never stays in the grave. Not only has it survived, it has thrived. It is the single most popular book in all of history. It has been the best-selling book in the world for years!

There is no way on earth to explain it. Which perhaps is the only explanation. The answer? The Bible's durability is not found on earth; it is found in heaven. For the millions who have tested its claims and claimed its promises, there is but one answer—the Bible is God's book and God's voice.

As you read it, you would be wise to give some thought to two questions. What is the purpose of the Bible? and How do I study the Bible? Time spent reflecting on these two issues will greatly enhance your Bible study.

What is the purpose of the Bible?

Let the Bible itself answer that question.

Since you were a child you have known the Holy Scriptures which are able to make you wise. And that wisdom leads to salvation through faith in Christ Jesus.

(2 Tim. 3:15)

The purpose of the Bible? Salvation. God's highest passion is to get his children home. His book, the Bible, describes his plan of salvation. The purpose of the Bible is to proclaim God's plan and passion to save his children.

That is the reason this book has endured through the centuries. It dares to tackle the toughest questions about life: Where do I go after I die? Is there a God? What do I do with my fears? The Bible offers answers to these crucial questions. It is the treasure map that leads us to God's highest treasure, eternal life.

But how do we use the Bible? Countless copies of Scripture sit unread on bookshelves and nightstands simply because people don't know how to read it. What can we do to make the Bible real in our lives?

The clearest answer is found in the words of Jesus.

"Ask," he promised, *"and God will give it to you. Search and you will find. Knock, and the door will open for you."*

(Matt. 7:7)

The first step in understanding the Bible is asking God to help us. We should read prayerfully. If anyone understands God's Word, it is because of God and not the reader.

But the Helper will teach you everything and will cause you to remember all that I told you. The Helper is the Holy Spirit whom the Father will send in my name.

(John 14:24)

Before reading the Bible, pray. Invite God to speak to you. Don't go to Scripture looking for your idea, go searching for his.

Not only should we read the Bible prayerfully, we should read it carefully. *Search and you will find* is the pledge. The Bible is not a newspaper to be skimmed but rather a mine to be quarried. *Search for it like silver, and hunt for it like hidden treasure. Then you will understand respect for the LORD, and you will find that you know God* (Prov. 2:4).

Any worthy find requires effort. The Bible is no exception. To understand the Bible you don't have to be brilliant, but you must be willing to roll up your sleeves and search.

Be a worker who is not ashamed and who uses the true teaching in the right way.

(2 Tim. 2:15)

Here's a practical point. Study the Bible a bit at a time. Hunger is not satisfied by eating twenty-one meals in one sitting once a week. The body needs a steady diet to remain strong. So does the soul. When God sent food to his people in the wilderness, he didn't provide loaves already made. Instead, he sent them manna in the shape of *thin flakes, like frost . . . on the desert ground* (Exod. 16:14).

God gave manna in limited portions.

God sends spiritual food the same way. He opens the heavens with just enough nutrients for today's hunger. He provides, *a command here, a command there. A rule here, a rule there. A little lesson here, a little lesson there* (Isa. 28:10).

Don't be discouraged if your reading reaps a small harvest. Some days a lesser portion is all that is needed. What is important is to search every day for that day's message. A steady diet of God's Word over a lifetime builds a healthy soul and mind.

A little girl returned from her first day at school. Her mom asked, "Did you learn anything?" "Apparently not enough," the girl responded, "I have to go back tomorrow and the next day and the next. . . ."

Such is the case with learning. And such is the case with Bible study. Understanding comes little by little over a lifetime.

There is a third step in understanding the Bible. After the asking and seeking comes the knocking. After you ask and search, then knock.

Knock, and the door will open for you.
(Matt. 7:7)

To knock is to stand at God's door. To make yourself available. To climb the steps, cross the porch, stand at the doorway, and volunteer. Knocking goes beyond the realm of thinking and into the realm of acting.

To knock is to ask, What can I do? How can I obey? Where can I go?

It's one thing to know what to do. It's another to do it. But for those who do it, those who choose to obey, a special reward awaits them.

The truly happy are those who carefully study God's perfect law that makes people free, and they continue to study it. They do not forget what they heard, but they obey what God's teaching says. Those who do this will be made happy.
(James 1:25)

What a promise. Happiness comes to those who do what they read! It's the same with medicine. If you only read the label but ignore the pills, it won't help. It's the same with food. If you only read the recipe but never cook, you won't be fed. And it's the same with the Bible. If you only read the words but never obey, you'll never know the joy God has promised.

Ask. Search. Knock. Simple, isn't it? Why don't you give it a try? If you do, you'll see why you are holding the most remarkable book in history.

MARK

INTRODUCTION

The drama of Mark's Gospel peaks in Caesarea Philippi.

It's a religious mecca. Every major religion can be found here. Temples dot the landscape. Priests stride the streets.

Jesus and his followers are here? Why? If Jesus preached a sermon, it's not recorded. If he performed a miracle, we don't know it. As far as we know, all he did was ask two questions.

The first, "Who do people say that I am?"

The disciples are quick to respond. They've overheard the chatter. "Some say you are John the Baptist. Others say you are Elijah, and others say you are one of the prophets."

Good answers. True answers. But wrong answers.

Jesus then turns and asks them the question. *The* question. "But who do you say that I am?"

He doesn't ask, "What do you think about what I've done." He asks, "Who do you say that I am."

He doesn't ask, "Who *did* you think I was when the crowds were great and the miracles were many?" He asks, "Who *do* you think I am. Here against the backdrop of religion. Me, a penniless itinerant surrounded by affluent temples. Who do you say I am?"

He doesn't ask, "Who do your friends think . . . Who do your parents think . . . Who do your peers think." He poses instead a starkly personal query, "Who do *you* think I am?"

The disciples aren't as quick to respond. One ducks his eyes. Another shuffles his feet. A third clears his throat. But Peter lifts his head. He lifts his head and looks at the Nazarene and speaks the words heaven has longed to hear. "You are the Christ."

You have been asked some important questions in your life:

Will you marry me?

Would you be interested in a transfer?

What would you think if I told you I was pregnant?

You've been asked some important questions. But the grandest of them is an anthill compared to the Everest found in the eighth chapter of Mark. *Who do you say that I am?*

LESSON ONE

COMPASSION

REFLECTION

Begin your study by sharing thoughts on this question.

1. Think of a time when you were hurting or in need. How did someone show you compassion?

_____

_____

_____

BIBLE READING

Read Mark 1:40–45 from the NCV or the NKJV.

NCV

⁴⁰A man with a skin disease came to Jesus. He fell to his knees and begged Jesus, "You can heal me if you will."

⁴¹Jesus felt sorry for the man, so he reached out his hand and touched him and said, "I will. Be healed!" ⁴²Immediately the disease left the man, and he was healed.

⁴³Jesus told the man to go away at once, but he warned him strongly, ⁴⁴"Don't tell anyone

NKJV

⁴⁰Now a leper came to Him, imploring Him, kneeling down to Him and saying to Him, "If You are willing, You can make me clean."

⁴¹Then Jesus, moved with compassion, stretched out His hand and touched him, and said to him, "I am willing; be cleansed." ⁴²As soon as He had spoken, immediately the leprosy left him, and he was cleansed. ⁴³And He strictly warned him and sent him away at once,

NCV

about this. But go and show yourself to the priest. And offer the gift Moses commanded for people who are made well. This will show the people what I have done." ⁴⁵The man left there, but he began to tell everyone that Jesus had healed him, and so he spread the news about Jesus. As a result, Jesus could not enter a town if people saw him. He stayed in places where nobody lived, but people came to him from everywhere.

NKJV

⁴⁴and said to him, "See that you say nothing to anyone; but go your way, show yourself to the priest, and offer for your cleansing those things which Moses commanded, as a testimony to them."

⁴⁵However, he went out and began to proclaim it freely, and to spread the matter, so that Jesus could no longer openly enter the city, but was outside in deserted places; and they came to Him from every direction.

DISCOVERY

Explore the Bible reading by discussing these questions.

2. What does the leper's statement reveal about his belief in Jesus?

_____

_____

_____

3. Jesus could have healed the leper simply by speaking to him. Why do you think Jesus reached out and touched him?

_____

_____

_____

4. Lepers were the outcasts of society, forced to live outside the city limits. Why did this leper approach Jesus?

_____

_____

_____

5. Why didn't the leper obey Jesus' request to keep quiet?

_____

_____

_____

6. Describe what the leper may have felt after Jesus touched and healed him?

_____

_____

_____

INSPIRATION

Here is an uplifting thought from the *Inspirational Study Bible.*

Jesus was a master at communicating love and personal acceptance. He did so when He blessed and held...little children. But another time His sensitivity to touch someone was even more graphic. This was when Jesus met a grown man's need for meaningful touch, a man who was barred by law from ever touching anyone again....

To touch a leper was unthinkable. Banishing lepers from society, people would not get within a stone's throw of them. (In fact, they would throw stones at them if they did come close!) ... With their open sores and dirty bandages, lepers were the last persons anyone would want to touch. Yet the first thing Christ did for this man was touch him.

Even before Jesus spoke to him, He reached out His hand and touched him. Can you imagine what that scene must have looked like? Think how this man must have longed for someone to touch him, not throw stones at him to drive him away. Jesus could have healed him first and then touched him. But recognizing his deepest need, Jesus stretched out His hand even before He spoke words of physical and spiritual healing.

(from *The Gift of the Blessing* by Gary Smalley and John Trent)

RESPONSE

Use these questions to share more deeply with each other.

7. Think of a time when you witnessed an act of compassion. Describe what you saw.

_____

_____

_____

8. Have you ever withheld compassion from someone in need? Why?

_____

_____

_____

9. How can you follow Jesus' example and show compassion even to those you find unattractive?

_____

_____

_____

PRAYER

Lift up our eyes, Father, that we might see our world as you see it. Teach us to build bridges between our hearts and those of people who need a friend or a helping hand. Help us respond as you respond to the hurts around us.

JOURNALING

Take a few moments to record your personal insights from this lesson.

What are some practical ways that I can reach out in compassion to those around me?

ADDITIONAL QUESTIONS

10. In what ways do you need Jesus' compassionate touch?

_____

_____

_____

11. What character traits does Jesus display in this story?

_____

_____

_____

12. Who are the "lepers" of today's society?

_____

_____

_____

For more Bible passages about compassion, see Matthew 8:15; 9:36; 14:14; 15:32; 20:34; Mark 10:13–16; Luke 7:13; 22:51.

To complete the book of Mark during this twelve-part study, read Mark 1:1–45.

ADDITIONAL THOUGHTS

LESSON TWO

HEALING AND FORGIVENESS

REFLECTION

Begin your study by sharing thoughts on this question.

1. Think of someone who has been healed physically, emotionally or spiritually. What were the circumstances surrounding that person's healing?

_____

_____

_____

BIBLE READING

Read Mark 2:1–12 from the NCV or the NKJV.

NCV

¹A few days later, when Jesus came back to Capernaum, the news spread that he was at home. ²Many people gathered together so that there was no room in the house, not even outside the door. And Jesus was teaching them God's message. ³Four people came, carrying a paralyzed man. ⁴Since they could not get to Jesus because of the crowd, they dug a hole in the roof right above where he was speaking.

NKJV

¹And again He entered Capernaum after some days, and it was heard that He was in the house. ²Immediately many gathered together, so that there was no longer room to receive them, not even near the door. And He preached the word to them. ³Then they came to Him, bringing a paralytic who was carried by four men. ⁴And when they could not come near Him because of the crowd, they uncovered the roof

NCV

When they got through, they lowered the mat with the paralyzed man on it. ⁵When Jesus saw the faith of these people, he said to the paralyzed man, "Young man, your sins are forgiven."

⁶Some of the teachers of the law were sitting there, thinking to themselves, ⁷"Why does this man say things like that? He is speaking as if he were God. Only God can forgive sins."

⁸Jesus knew immediately what these teachers of the law were thinking. So he said to them, "Why are you thinking these things? ⁹Which is easier: to tell this paralyzed man, 'Your sins are forgiven,' or to tell him, 'Stand up. Take your mat and walk'? ¹⁰But I will prove to you that the Son of Man has authority on earth to forgive sins." So Jesus said to the paralyzed man, ¹¹"I tell you, stand up, take your mat, and go home." ¹²Immediately the paralyzed man stood up, took his mat, and walked out while everyone was watching him.

The people were amazed and praised God. They said, "We have never seen anything like this!"

NKJV

where He was. So when they had broken through, they let down the bed on which the paralytic was lying.

⁵When Jesus saw their faith, He said to the paralytic, "Son, your sins are forgiven you."

⁶And some of the scribes were sitting there and reasoning in their hearts, ⁷"Why does this Man speak blasphemies like this? Who can forgive sins but God alone?"

⁸But immediately, when Jesus perceived in His spirit that they reasoned thus within themselves, He said to them, "Why do you reason about these things in your hearts? ⁹Which is easier, to say to the paralytic, 'Your sins are forgiven you,' or to say, 'Arise, take up your bed and walk'? ¹⁰But that you may know that the Son of Man has power on earth to forgive sins"—He said to the paralytic, ¹¹"I say to you, arise, take up your bed, and go to your house." ¹²Immediately he arose, took up the bed, and went out in the presence of them all, so that all were amazed and glorified God, saying, "We never saw anything like this!"

DISCOVERY

Explore the Bible reading by discussing these questions.

2. What risks did the men take who carried the paralytic?

   _____

   _____

   _____

3. Why were the scribes upset when Jesus forgave the paralytic's sins?

   _____

   _____

   _____

4. Why did Jesus forgive the paralytic's sins before healing his body?

   _____

   _____

   _____

5. How did the people respond to the miracle? How is their response different from the way people respond to God's work today?

   _____

   _____

   _____

6. What does it mean to be healed spiritually?

_____

_____

_____

INSPIRATION

Here is an uplifting thought from the *Inspirational Study Bible*.

Whether he was born paralyzed or became paralyzed—the end result was the same: total dependence on others....When people looked at him, they didn't see the man; they saw a body in need of a miracle. That's not what Jesus saw, but that's what the people saw. And that's certainly what his friends saw. So they did what any of us would do for a friend. They tried to get him some help....

By the time his friends arrived at the place, the house was full. People jammed the doorways. Kids sat in the windows. Others peeked over shoulders. How would this small band of friends ever attract Jesus' attention? They had to make a choice. Do we go in or give up?

What would have happened had the friends given up? What if they had shrugged their shoulders and mumbled something about the crowd being big and dinner getting cold and turned and left? After all, they had done a good deed in coming this far. Who could fault them for turning back? You can only do so much for somebody. But these friends hadn't done enough.

One said that he had an idea. The four huddled over the paralytic and listened to the plan to climb to the top of the house, cut through the roof, and lower their friend down with their sashes.

It was risky—they could fall. It was dangerous—*he* could fall. It was unorthodox—de-roofing is antisocial. It was intrusive—Jesus was busy. But it was their only chance to see Jesus. So they climbed to the roof.

Faith does these things. Faith does the unexpected. And faith gets God's attention....

Jesus was moved by the scene of faith. So he applauds—if not with his hands, at least with his heart. And not only does he applaud, he blesses. And we witness a divine loveburst.

The friends want him to heal their friend. But Jesus won't settle for a simple healing of the body—he wants to heal the soul. He leapfrogs the physical and deals with the spiritual. To heal the body is temporal; to heal the soul is eternal....So strong was his love for this crew of faith that he went beyond their appeal and went straight to the cross.

Jesus already knows the cost of grace. He already knows the price of forgiveness. But he offers it anyway. Love bursts in his heart....

And though we can't hear it here, the angels can hear him there. All of heaven must pause as another burst of love declares the only words that really matter: "Your sins are forgiven."

(from *He Still Moves Stones*
by Max Lucado)

RESPONSE

Use these questions to share more deeply with each other.

7. In what ways can you identify with the paralytic?

_____

_____

_____

8. Think of a time when you experienced Christ's healing touch in your life. How did it affect you?

_____

_____

_____

9. Many people need God's spiritual, emotional, or physical healing. In what ways can you share God's love and forgiveness with them?

_____

_____

_____

PRAYER

Father, sometimes we are afraid that we've done something unforgivable, afraid that we've made you angry. But Father, your Word teaches us that you will forgive us and that there's no sin too deep for your hand of forgiveness to reach.

JOURNALING

Take a few moments to record your personal insights from this lesson.

In what areas of my life has Christ's power to forgive and heal been most evident?

ADDITIONAL QUESTIONS

10. Jesus' attitude and the Pharisees' attitude varied greatly. What does this story illustrate about attitudes that honor God?

_____

_____

_____

11. The paralytic's friends displayed great determination in their mission. Was this more important for them or for the paralytic?

_____

_____

_____

12. When has God exceeded your expectations and provided more than you expected?

_____

_____

_____

For more Bible passages about healing and forgiveness, see Matthew 7:7; 15:29–31; Mark 9:20–24; John 9:1–12; Romans 6; Titus 3:1–7.

To complete the book of Mark during this twelve-part study, read Mark 2:1–3:35.

LESSON THREE

RESPONDING TO GOD'S WORD

REFLECTION

Begin your study by sharing thoughts on this question.

1. Have you ever planted seeds and watched them grow? What impresses you most about this growth process?

_____

_____

_____

BIBLE READING

Read Mark 4:1–20 from the NCV or the NKJV.

NCV

¹Again Jesus began teaching by the lake. A great crowd gathered around him, so he sat down in a boat near the shore. All the people stayed on the shore close to the water. ²Jesus taught them many things, using stories. He said, ³"Listen! A farmer went out to plant his seed. ⁴While he was planting, some seed fell by the road, and the birds came and ate it up. ⁵Some seed fell on rocky ground where there

NKJV

¹And again He began to teach by the sea. And a great multitude was gathered to Him, so that He got into a boat and sat in it on the sea; and the whole multitude was on the land facing the sea. ²Then He taught them many things by parables, and said to them in His teaching: ³"Listen! Behold, a sower went out to sow. ⁴And it happened, as he sowed, that some seed fell by the wayside; and the birds of the air came

NCV

wasn't much dirt. That seed grew very fast, because the ground was not deep. ⁶But when the sun rose, the plants dried up because they did not have deep roots. ⁷Some other seed fell among thorny weeds, which grew and choked the good plants. So those plants did not produce a crop. ⁸Some other seed fell on good ground and began to grow. It got taller and produced a crop. Some plants made thirty times more, some made sixty times more, and some made a hundred times more."

⁹Then Jesus said, "You people who can hear me, listen!"

¹⁰Later, when Jesus was alone, the twelve apostles and others around him asked him about the stories.

¹¹Jesus said, "You can know the secret about the kingdom of God. But to other people I tell everything by using stories ¹²so that:

'They will look and look, but they will not
   learn.
They will listen and listen, but they will
   not understand.
If they did learn and understand,
   they would come back to me and be
   forgiven.' "

¹³Then Jesus said to his followers, "Don't you understand this story? If you don't, how will you understand any story? ¹⁴The farmer is like a person who plants God's message in people. ¹⁵Sometimes the teaching falls on the road. This is like the people who hear the teaching of God, but Satan quickly comes and takes away the teaching that was planted in them. ¹⁶Others are like the seed planted on rocky ground. They hear the teaching and quickly accept it with joy.

NKJV

and devoured it. ⁵Some fell on stony ground, where it did not have much earth; and immediately it sprang up because it had no depth of earth. ⁶But when the sun was up it was scorched, and because it had no root it withered away. ⁷And some seed fell among thorns; and the thorns grew up and choked it, and it yielded no crop. ⁸But other seed fell on good ground and yielded a crop that sprang up, increased and produced: some thirtyfold, some sixty, and some a hundred."

⁹And He said to them, "He who has ears to hear, let him hear!"

¹⁰But when He was alone, those around Him with the twelve asked Him about the parable. ¹¹And He said to them, "To you it has been given to know the mystery of the kingdom of God; but to those who are outside, all things come in parables, ¹²so that

'Seeing they may see and not perceive,
And hearing they may hear and not
   understand;
Lest they should turn,
And their sins be forgiven them.'"

¹³And He said to them, "Do you not understand this parable? How then will you understand all the parables? ¹⁴The sower sows the word. ¹⁵And these are the ones by the wayside where the word is sown. When they hear, Satan comes immediately and takes away the word that was sown in their hearts. ¹⁶These likewise are the ones sown on stony ground who, when they hear the word, immediately receive it with gladness; ¹⁷and they have no root in themselves,

NCV

[17]But since they don't allow the teaching to go deep into their lives, they keep it only a short time. When trouble or persecution comes because of the teaching they accepted, they quickly give up. [18]Others are like the seed planted among the thorny weeds. They hear the teaching, [19]but the worries of this life, the temptation of wealth, and many other evil desires keep the teaching from growing and producing fruit in their lives. [20]Others are like the seed planted in the good ground. They hear the teaching and accept it. Then they grow and produce fruit—sometimes thirty times more, sometimes sixty times more, and sometimes a hundred times more."

NKJV

and so endure only for a time. Afterward, when tribulation or persecution arises for the word's sake, immediately they stumble. [18]Now these are the ones sown among thorns; they are the ones who hear the word, [19]and the cares of this world, the deceitfulness of riches, and the desires for other things entering in choke the word, and it becomes unfruitful. [20]But these are the ones sown on good ground, those who hear the word, accept it, and bear fruit: some thirtyfold, some sixty, and some a hundred."

DISCOVERY

Explore the Bible reading by discussing these questions.

2. What does each type of soil in the story represent?

_____

_____

_____

3. What do the sower and the seed represent?

_____

_____

_____

4. How does the story of the seeds parallel our spiritual lives?

_____

_____

_____

5. How will our lives change when we begin to bear fruit?

_____

_____

_____

6. List some examples of what a fruitful Christian might do.

_____

_____

_____

INSPIRATION

Here is an uplifting thought from the *Inspirational Study Bible*.

Think about the first time you ever saw him. Think about your first encounter with Christ. Robe yourself in that moment. Resurrect the relief. Recall the purity. Summon forth the passion. Can you remember?

I can. 1965. A red-headed ten-year-old with a tornado of freckles sits in a Bible class on a Wednesday night. What I remember of the class are scenes—school desks with initials carved in them. A blackboard. A dozen or so kids, some listening, some not. A teacher wearing a suit coat too tight to button around his robust belly.

He is talking about Jesus. He is explaining the cross. I know I had heard it before, but that night I heard it for sure. "You can't save yourself, you need a savior." I can't explain why it connected that night as opposed to another, but it did. He simply articulated what I was beginning to understand—I was lost—and he explained what I needed—a redeemer. From that night on, my heart belonged to Jesus.

Many would argue that a ten-year-old is too young for such a decision. And they may be right. All I know is that I never made a more earnest decision in my life. I didn't know much about God, but what I knew was enough. I knew I wanted to go to heaven. And I knew I couldn't do it alone.

No one had to tell me to be happy. No one had to tell me to tell others. They couldn't keep me quiet. I told all my friends at school. I put a bumper sticker on my bicycle.

(from *Six Hours One Friday*
by Max Lucado)

RESPONSE

Use these questions to share more deeply with each other.

7. At different times in our lives our "soil type" may change. Which soil type currently represents your response to God and his Word?

_____

_____

_____

8. What tactics does Satan use to prevent us from hearing and understanding God's Word?

_____

_____

_____

9. What "thorns" may be choking your ability to bear fruit?

_____

_____

_____

PRAYER

Father, you have given us such a great promise, the promise of salvation. Forgive us when we let the thorny desires and cares of this world choke out our desire to serve you.

JOURNALING

Take a few moments to record your personal insights from this lesson.

How can I weed out the "thorns" that hinder my spiritual growth?

ADDITIONAL QUESTIONS

10. In what ways are you trying to nourish the spiritual "seed" God has planted in your life?

_____

_____

_____

11. What is your church doing to promote spiritual growth?

_____

_____

_____

12. What can you do to help the seed take root in others?

_____

_____

_____

For more Bible passages about responding to God's Word, see Psalm 119:99, 138; John 20:22–29; Acts 2:38–41; Galatians 5:22; Ephesians 6:17; 1 Peter 2:2.

To complete the book of Mark during this twelve-part study, read Mark 4:1–34.

LESSON FOUR

FAITH THROUGH TRIALS

REFLECTION

Begin your study by sharing thoughts on this question.

1. Think back to the worst storm you can remember. What were your feelings throughout the storm?

_____

_____

_____

BIBLE READING

Read Mark 4:35–41 from the NCV or the NKJV.

NCV

[35]That evening, Jesus said to his followers, "Let's go across the lake." [36]Leaving the crowd behind, they took him in the boat just as he was. There were also other boats with them. [37]A very strong wind came up on the lake. The waves came over the sides and into the boat so that it was already full of water. [38]Jesus was at the back of the boat, sleeping with his head on a cushion. His followers woke him and said, "Teacher, don't you care that we are drowning!"

NKJV

[35]On the same day, when evening had come, He said to them, "Let us cross over to the other side." [36]Now when they had left the multitude, they took Him along in the boat as He was. And other little boats were also with Him. [37]And a great windstorm arose, and the waves beat into the boat, so that it was already filling. [38]But He was in the stern, asleep on a pillow. And they awoke Him and said to Him, "Teacher, do You not care that we are perishing?"

NCV

³⁹Jesus stood up and commanded the wind and said to the waves, "Quiet! Be still!" Then the wind stopped, and it became completely calm.

⁴⁰Jesus said to his followers, "Why are you afraid? Do you still have no faith?"

⁴¹The followers were very afraid and asked each other, "Who is this? Even the wind and the waves obey him!"

NKJV

³⁹Then He arose and rebuked the wind, and said to the sea, "Peace, be still!" And the wind ceased and there was a great calm. ⁴⁰But He said to them, "Why are you so fearful? How is it that you have no faith?" ⁴¹And they feared exceedingly, and said to one another, "Who can this be, that even the wind and the sea obey Him!"

DISCOVERY

Explore the Bible reading by discussing these questions.

2. Why were the disciples afraid of the storm?

_____

_____

_____

3. What does this experience reveal about the disciples?

_____

_____

_____

4. Why do you think Jesus calmed the storm?

_____

_____

_____

5. What were the disciples' attitudes about Jesus after he calmed the storm?

_____

_____

_____

6. Do you have the tendency to remain afraid rather than ask Jesus for help? Why?

_____

_____

_____

INSPIRATION

Here is an uplifting thought from the *Inspirational Study Bible.*

If you lose your faith, you will probably do so gradually. In tiny increments you will get spiritually sloppy. You will let a few days slip by without consulting your compass. Your sails will go untrimmed. Your rigging will go unprepared. And worst of all, you will forget to anchor your boat. And, before your know it, you'll be bouncing from wave to wave in stormy seas....

Stability in the storm comes not from seeking a new message, but from understanding an old one. The most reliable anchor points are not recent discoveries, but are time-tested truths that have held their ground against the winds of change....

Attach your soul to these boulders and no wave is big enough to wash you under.

(from *Six Hours One Friday*
by Max Lucado)

RESPONSE

Use these questions to share more deeply with each other.

7. In what ways can you identify with the fearful disciples?

_____

_____

_____

8. What is the purpose of the "life storms" we experience?

_____

_____

_____

9. How have you reacted to the "life storms" you've experienced?

_____

_____

_____

PRAYER

Father, teach us to set our hopes on heaven and to hold firmly to the promise of eternal life. May your Holy Word be a soothing medicine to our wounded hearts.

JOURNALING

Take a few moments to record your personal insights from this lesson.

What can I do to face future "life storms" more confidently?

ADDITIONAL QUESTIONS

10. How has God proven himself faithful to you during a difficult time?

_____

_____

_____

11. What does this passage teach you about Jesus?

_____

_____

_____

12. How would you encourage someone who is experiencing a troubling time?

_____

_____

_____

For more Bible passages about enduring trials, see Matthew 11:28–30;
John 15:18; 16:33; Romans 5:1–5; 8:28; 2 Corinthians 6:3–13; Philippians 3:7–11;
James 1:2–4.

To complete the book of Mark during this twelve-part study, read Mark 4:35–5:20.

ADDITIONAL THOUGHTS

_____

_____

_____

_____

_____

_____

_____

_____

_____

_____

_____

_____

_____

_____

_____

_____

_____

_____

_____

LESSON FIVE

STEP OUT IN FAITH

REFLECTION

Begin your study by sharing thoughts on this question.

1. Think of a time when you took a step of faith. What did you do and how did God respond?

_____

_____

_____

BIBLE READING

Read Mark 5:21–42 from the NCV or the NKJV.

NCV

²¹When Jesus went in the boat back to the other side of the lake, a large crowd gathered around him there. ²²A leader of the synagogue, named Jairus, came there, saw Jesus, and fell at his feet. ²³He begged Jesus, saying again and again, "My daughter is dying. Please come and put your hands on her so she will be healed and will live." ²⁴So Jesus went with him.

NKJV

²¹Now when Jesus had crossed over again by boat to the other side, a great multitude gathered to Him; and He was by the sea. ²²And behold, one of the rulers of the synagogue came, Jairus by name. And when he saw Him, he fell at His feet ²³and begged Him earnestly, saying, "My little daughter lies at the point of death. Come and lay Your hands on her, that she

NCV

A large crowd followed Jesus and pushed very close around him. [25]Among them was a woman who had been bleeding for twelve years. [26]She had suffered very much from many doctors and had spent all the money she had, but instead of improving, she was getting worse. [27]When the woman heard about Jesus, she came up behind him in the crowd and touched his coat. [28]She thought, "If I can just touch his clothes, I will be healed." [29]Instantly her bleeding stopped, and she felt in her body that she was healed from her disease.

[30]At once Jesus felt power go out from him. So he turned around in the crowd and asked, "Who touched my clothes?"

[31]His followers said, "Look at how many people are pushing against you! And you ask, 'Who touched me?'"

[32]But Jesus continued looking around to see who had touched him. [33]The woman, knowing that she was healed, came and fell at Jesus' feet. Shaking with fear, she told him the whole truth. [34]Jesus said to her, "Dear woman, you are made well because you believed. Go in peace; be healed of your disease."

[35]While Jesus was still speaking, some people came from the house of the synagogue leader. They said, "Your daughter is dead. There is no need to bother the teacher anymore."

[36]But Jesus paid no attention to what they said. He told the synagogue leader, "Don't be afraid; just believe."

[37]Jesus let only Peter, James, and John the brother of James go with him. [38]When they came to the house of the synagogue leader, Jesus found many people there making lots of

NKJV

may be healed, and she will live." [24]So Jesus went with him, and a great multitude followed Him and thronged Him.

[25]Now a certain woman had a flow of blood for twelve years, [26]and had suffered many things from many physicians. She had spent all that she had and was no better, but rather grew worse. [27]When she heard about Jesus, she came behind Him in the crowd and touched His garment. [28]For she said, "If only I may touch His clothes, I shall be made well."

[29]Immediately the fountain of her blood was dried up, and she felt in her body that she was healed of the affliction. [30]And Jesus, immediately knowing in Himself that power had gone out of Him, turned around in the crowd and said, "Who touched My clothes?"

[31]But His disciples said to Him, "You see the multitude thronging You, and You say, 'Who touched Me?'"

[32]And He looked around to see her who had done this thing. [33]But the woman, fearing and trembling, knowing what had happened to her, came and fell down before Him and told Him the whole truth. [34]And He said to her, "Daughter, your faith has made you well. Go in peace, and be healed of your affliction."

[35]While He was still speaking, some came from the ruler of the synagogue's house who said, "Your daughter is dead. Why trouble the Teacher any further?"

[36]As soon as Jesus heard the word that was spoken, He said to the ruler of the synagogue, "Do not be afraid; only believe." [37]And He permitted no one to follow Him except Peter, James, and John the brother of James. [38]Then

NCV

noise and crying loudly. ³⁹Jesus entered the house and said to them, "Why are you crying and making so much noise? The child is not dead, only asleep." ⁴⁰But they laughed at him. So, after throwing them out of the house, Jesus took the child's father and mother and his three followers into the room where the child was. ⁴¹Taking hold of the girl's hand, he said to her, "Talitha, koum!" (This means, "Young girl, I tell you to stand up!") ⁴²At once the girl stood right up and began walking. (She was twelve years old.) Everyone was completely amazed.

NKJV

He came to the house of the ruler of the synagogue, and saw a tumult and those who wept and wailed loudly. ³⁹When He came in, He said to them, "Why make this commotion and weep? The child is not dead, but sleeping."

⁴⁰And they ridiculed Him. But when He had put them all outside, He took the father and the mother of the child, and those who were with Him, and entered where the child was lying. ⁴¹Then He took the child by the hand, and said to her, "Talitha, cumi," which is translated, "Little girl, I say to you, arise." ⁴²Immediately the girl arose and walked, for she was twelve years of age. And they were overcome with great amazement.

DISCOVERY

Explore the Bible reading by discussing these questions.

2. Why is it surprising that Jairus publicly approached Jesus and begged him to heal his daughter?

_____

_____

_____

3. What made it difficult for this woman to approach Jesus?

_____

_____

_____

4. How do you think Jairus felt when Jesus stopped to heal the woman?

_____

_____

_____

5. Why do you suppose Jesus stopped to point out the woman?

_____

_____

_____

6. What does the story of Jairus and the woman reveal about faith?

_____

_____

_____

INSPIRATION

Here is an uplifting thought from the *Inspirational Study Bible.*

A chronic menstrual disorder. A perpetual issue of blood. Such a condition would be difficult for any woman of any era. But for a Jewess, nothing could be worse. No part of her life was left unaffected.

Sexually . . . she could not touch her husband.

Maternally . . . she could not bear children.

Domestically . . . anything she touched was considered unclean. No washing dishes. No sweeping floors.

Spiritually . . . she was not allowed to enter the temple.

She was physically exhausted and socially ostracized.

She had sought help "under the care of many doctors". . . .

She was a bruised reed. She awoke daily in a body that no one wanted. She is down to her last prayer. And on the day we encounter her, she's about to pray it.

By the time she gets to Jesus, he is surrounded by people. He's on his way to help the daughter of Jairus, the most important man in the community. What are the odds that he will interrupt an urgent mission with a high official to help the likes of her? Very few. But what are the odds that she will survive if she doesn't take a chance? Fewer still. So she takes a chance.

"If I can just touch his clothes", she thinks, "I will be healed."

Risky decision. To touch him, she will have to touch the people. If one of them recognizes her . . . But what choice does she have? She has no money, no clout, no friends, no solutions. All she has is a crazy hunch that Jesus can help and a high hope that he will. . . .

There was no guarantee, of course. She hoped he'd respond . . . she longed for it . . . but she didn't know if he would. All she knew was that he was good. That's faith.

Faith is not the belief that God will do what you want. Faith is the belief that God will do what is right.

"Blessed are the dirt-poor, nothing-to-give, trapped-in-a-corner, destitute, diseased," Jesus said, "for theirs is the kingdom of heaven" (Matt. 5:6, my translation).

God's economy is upside down (or rightside up and ours is upside down!) God says that the more hopeless your circumstance, the more likely your salvation. The greater your cares, the more genuine your prayers. The darker the room, the greater the need for light.

A healthy lady never would have appreciated the power of a touch of the hem of his robe. But this woman was sick . . . and when her dilemma met his dedication, a miracle occurred.

Her part in the healing was very small. All she did was extend her arm through the crowd.

"If only I can touch him." . . .

Healing begins when we do something. Healing begins when we reach out. Healing starts when we take a step.

(from *He still Moves Stones*
by Max Lucado)

RESPONSE

Use these questions to share more deeply with each other.

7. In what ways can you identify with the bleeding woman?

8. Think of a time when you found it difficult to step out in faith. Why was it difficult for you?

9. In what area of life do you need to experience Christ's power?

PRAYER

Father, you promise strength and hope to meet life's problems for those who are faithful. Give that strength to those whose anxieties have buried their dreams, whose illnesses have hospitalized their hopes, whose burdens are bigger than their shoulders.

JOURNALING

Take a few moments to record your personal insights from this lesson.

What steps can I take to strengthen my faith?

ADDITIONAL QUESTIONS

10. What does this story teach you about Jesus' compassion?

11. Jesus comforted Jairus by saying "Don't be afraid, only believe." How are these words applicable to your life?

12. Many people touched Jesus as he passed by. Why did Jesus' power affect this woman and not others?

For more Bible passages about stepping out in faith, see Genesis 12:2–9; 22:1–19; Joshua 6; Daniel 3; Matthew 7:7; Luke 17:6; Hebrews 11:1, 7–12.

To complete the book of Mark during this twelve-part study, read Mark 5:21–43.

LESSON SIX

TESTING FAITH

REFLECTION

Begin your study by sharing thoughts on this question.

1. Think of a time when you were endangered by a terrible storm or natural disaster. How did you feel while you were in danger?

_____

_____

_____

BIBLE READING

Read Mark 6:45–51 from the NCV or the NKJV.

NCV	NKJV
⁴⁵Immediately Jesus told his followers to get into the boat and go ahead of him to Bethsaida across the lake. He stayed there to send the people home. ⁴⁶After sending them away, he went into the hills to pray. ⁴⁷That night, the boat was in the middle of the lake, and Jesus was alone on the land. ⁴⁸He saw his followers struggling hard to row the boat, because the wind was blowing against	⁴⁵Immediately He made His disciples get into the boat and go before Him to the other side, to Bethsaida, while He sent the multitude away. ⁴⁶And when He had sent them away, He departed to the mountain to pray. ⁴⁷Now when evening came, the boat was in the middle of the sea; and He was alone on the land. ⁴⁸Then He saw them straining at rowing, for the wind was against them. Now about the fourth watch of

NCV	**NKJV**
them. Between three and six o'clock in the morning, Jesus came to them, walking on the water, and he wanted to walk past the boat. ⁴⁹But when they saw him walking on the water, they thought he was a ghost and cried out. ⁵⁰They all saw him and were afraid. But quickly Jesus spoke to them and said, "Have courage! It is I. Do not be afraid." ⁵¹Then he got into the boat with them, and the wind became calm. The followers were greatly amazed.	the night He came to them, walking on the sea, and would have passed them by. ⁴⁹And when they saw Him walking on the sea, they supposed it was a ghost, and cried out; ⁵⁰for they all saw Him and were troubled. But immediately He talked with them and said to them, "Be of good cheer! It is I; do not be afraid." ⁵¹Then He went up into the boat to them, and the wind ceased. And they were greatly amazed in themselves beyond measure, and marveled.

DISCOVERY

Explore the Bible reading by discussing these questions.

2. Why didn't Jesus go with the disciples in the boat?

_____

_____

_____

3. What prevented the disciples from recognizing Jesus?

_____

_____

_____

4. What was Jesus trying to teach the disciples through this experience?

_____

_____

_____

5. What can you learn from the disciples' experience?

_____

_____

_____

6. Why does God test our faith?

_____

_____

_____

INSPIRATION

Here is an uplifting thought from the *Inspirational Study Bible.*

Children love to swing. There's nothing like it. Thrusting your feet toward the sky, leaning so far backward that everything looks upside down. Spinning trees, a stomach that jumps into your throat. Ah, swinging....

I learned a lot about trust on a swing. As a child, I only trusted certain people to push my swing. If I was being pushed by people I trusted (like Dad or Mom), they could do anything they wanted. They could twist me, turn me, stop me ...I loved it! I loved it because I trusted the person pushing me. But let a stranger push my swing (which often happened at family reunions and Fourth of July picnics), and it was *hang on, baby!* Who knew what this newcomer would do? When a stranger pushes your swing, you tense up, ball up, and hang on....

We live in a stormy world. At this writing, wars rage in both hemispheres of our globe. World conflict is threatening all humanity. Jobs are getting scarce. Money continues to get tight. Families are coming apart at the seams.

Everywhere I look, private storms occur. Family deaths, strained marriages, broken hearts, lonely evenings. We must remember who is pushing the swing. We must put our trust in him. We can't grow fearful. He won't let us tumble out.

Who pushes your swing? In the right hands, you can find peace ...even in the storm.

(from *On the Anvil*
by Max Lucado)

RESPONSE

Use these questions to share more deeply with each other.

7. In what ways has your faith been tested?

_____

_____

_____

8. How has Jesus responded to you in your test of faith?

_____

_____

_____

9. In their moment of greatest fear, Jesus calmed the disciples with words of assurance about his identity. How does knowing Jesus help in times of testing?

_____

_____

_____

PRAYER

Father, forgive us for the times that we have questioned you. Forgive us for the times we have doubted you. Forgive us for the times we've shaken our heads and pounded our fists against the earth and cried, "Where are you?" For Father, we know that you have been here—you've carried us through the valley, and you've given us strength.

JOURNALING

Take a few moments to record your personal insights from this lesson.

When testing comes, how can I remind myself that Jesus is always there, even if I can't "see" him?

ADDITIONAL QUESTIONS

10. What can you do to strengthen your faith for times of testing?

_____

_____

_____

11. How have the victorious experiences of others helped your faith grow?

_____

_____

_____

12. In what ways can your testing be a tool of evangelism?

_____

_____

_____

For more Bible passages about testing faith, see Psalm 112:8; John 16:33; 18:15–18; 18:25–27; 1 Corinthians 16:13; Hebrews 11:7–12.

To complete the book of Mark during this twelve-part study, read Mark 6:1–56.

ADDITIONAL THOUGHTS

LESSON SEVEN

GOD'S TRUTH vs. TRADITION

REFLECTION

Begin your study by sharing thoughts on this question.

1. Which of your family traditions would be difficult to change? Why?

_____

_____

_____

BIBLE READING

Read Mark 7:1–23 from the NCV or the NKJV.

NCV

¹When some Pharisees and some teachers of the law came from Jerusalem, they gathered around Jesus. ²They saw that some of Jesus' followers ate food with hands that were not clean, that is, they hadn't washed them. ³ (The Pharisees and all the Jews never eat before washing their hands in a special way according to their unwritten laws. ⁴And when they buy something in the market, they never eat it until they wash themselves in a special way. They

NKJV

¹Then the Pharisees and some of the scribes came together to Him, having come from Jerusalem. ²Now when they saw some of His disciples eat bread with defiled, that is, with unwashed hands, they found fault. ³For the Pharisees and all the Jews do not eat unless they wash their hands in a special way, holding the tradition of the elders. ⁴When they come from the marketplace, they do not eat unless they wash. And there are many other things

NCV

also follow many other unwritten laws, such as the washing of cups, pitchers, and pots.)

⁵The Pharisees and the teachers of the law said to Jesus, "Why don't your followers obey the unwritten laws which have been handed down to us? Why do your followers eat their food with hands that are not clean?"

⁶Jesus answered, "Isaiah was right when he spoke about you hypocrites. He wrote,
'These people show honor to me with
 words,
 but their hearts are far from me.
⁷Their worship of me is worthless.
 The things they teach are nothing but
 human rules.'
⁸You have stopped following the commands of God, and you follow only human teachings."

⁹Then Jesus said to them, "You cleverly ignore the commands of God so you can follow your own teachings. ¹⁰Moses said, 'Honor your father and your mother,' and 'Anyone who says cruel things to his father or mother must be put to death.' ¹¹But you say a person can tell his father or mother, 'I have something I could use to help you, but it is Corban—a gift to God.' ¹²You no longer let that person use that money for his father or his mother. ¹³By your own rules, which you teach people, you are rejecting what God said. And you do many things like that."

¹⁴After Jesus called the crowd to him again, he said, "Every person should listen to me and understand what I am saying. ¹⁵⁻¹⁶There is nothing people put into their bodies that makes them unclean. People are made unclean by the things that come out of them."

¹⁷When Jesus left the people and went into

NKJV

which they have received and hold, like the washing of cups, pitchers, copper vessels, and couches.

⁵Then the Pharisees and scribes asked Him, "Why do Your disciples not walk according to the tradition of the elders, but eat bread with unwashed hands?"

⁶He answered and said to them, "Well did Isaiah prophesy of you hypocrites, as it is written:

'This people honors Me with their lips,
 But their heart is far from Me.
⁷And in vain they worship Me,
 Teaching as doctrines the commandments
 of men.'

⁸"For laying aside the commandment of God, you hold the tradition of men—the washing of pitchers and cups, and many other such things you do."

⁹He said to them, "All too well you reject the commandment of God, that you may keep your tradition. ¹⁰For Moses said, 'Honor your father and your mother'; and, 'He who curses father or mother, let him be put to death.' ¹¹But you say, 'If a man says to his father or mother, "Whatever profit you might have received from me is Corban"—' (that is, a gift to God), ¹²then you no longer let him do anything for his father or his mother, ¹³making the word of God of no effect through your tradition which you have handed down. And many such things you do."

¹⁴When He had called all the multitude to Himself, He said to them, "Hear Me, everyone, and understand: ¹⁵There is nothing that enters

NCV

the house, his followers asked him about this story. [18]Jesus said, "Do you still not understand? Surely you know that nothing that enters someone from the outside can make that person unclean. [19]It does not go into the mind, but into the stomach. Then it goes out of the body." (When Jesus said this, he meant that no longer was any food unclean for people to eat.)

[20]And Jesus said, "The things that come out of people are the things that make them unclean. [21]All these evil things begin inside people, in the mind: evil thoughts, sexual sins, stealing, murder, adultery, [22]greed, evil actions, lying, doing sinful things, jealousy, speaking evil of others, pride, and foolish living. [23]All these evil things come from inside and make people unclean."

NKJV

a man from outside which can defile him; but the things which come out of him, those are the things that defile a man. [16]If anyone has ears to hear, let him hear!"

[17]When He had entered a house away from the crowd, His disciples asked Him concerning the parable. [18]So He said to them, "Are you thus without understanding also? Do you not perceive that whatever enters a man from outside cannot defile him, [19]because it does not enter his heart but his stomach, and is eliminated, thus purifying all foods?" [20]And He said, "What comes out of a man, that defiles a man. [21]For from within, out of the heart of men, proceed evil thoughts, adulteries, fornications, murders, [22]thefts, covetousness, wickedness, deceit, lewdness, an evil eye, blasphemy, pride, foolishness. [23]All these evil things come from within and defile a man."

DISCOVERY

Explore the Bible reading by discussing these questions.

2. According to Jewish tradition, what did the disciples do wrong?

_____

_____

_____

3. What did Jesus find so hypocritical about the Pharisees' and their traditions?

_____

_____

_____

4. What was the meaning of Jesus' parable?

_____

_____

_____

5. Why didn't the disciples understand the parable?

_____

_____

_____

6. Why was it easier to follow religious rules rather than to develop an intimate relationship with God?

_____

_____

_____

INSPIRATION

Here is an uplifting thought from the *Inspirational Study Bible*.

When my family lived in Rio de Janiero, I owned a ham radio. I kept it in the utility room on top of the freezer. When we traveled, I always unplugged the radio and disconnected the antenna.

Once, when we were leaving for a week-long trip, I remembered I hadn't unplugged the radio. I ran back in the house, pulled the plug, and dashed out again.

But I pulled the wrong plug. I unplugged the freezer.... For seven days, then, a freezer full of food sat in a sweltering apartment with the power off.

When we came home, . . . guess who got fingered as the one who had unplugged the freezer—and who therefore would be responsible for cleaning it? You got it. So I got to work.

What is the best way to clean out a rotten interior? I knew exactly what to do. I got a rag and a bucket of soapy water and began cleaning the outside of the appliance. I was sure the odor would disappear with a good shine, so I polished and buffed and wiped. When I was through, the freezer could have passed a Marine boot-camp inspection. It was sparkling.

But when I opened the door, that freezer was revolting.

(Are you wondering, "Now what kind of fool would do that?" Read on and you'll see.)

No problem, I thought. I knew what to do. This freezer needs some friends. I'd stink, too, if I had the social life of a machine in a utility room. So, I threw a party. I invited all the appliances from the neighborhood kitchens.

It was hard work, but we filled our apartment with refrigerators, stoves, microwaves, and washing machines. It was a great party. A couple of toasters recognized each other from the appliance store. Everyone played pin the plug on the socket and had a few laughs about limited warranties. The blenders were the hit, though; they really mixed well.

I was sure the social interaction would cure the inside of my freezer, but I was wrong. I opened it up, and the stink was even worse!

Now what?

I had an idea. If a polish job wouldn't do it and social life didn't help, I'd give the freezer some status!

I bought a Mercedes sticker and stuck it on the door. I painted a paisley tie down the front. I put a "Save the Whales" bumper sticker on the rear and installed a cellular phone on the side. That freezer was classy. It was stylish. It was ... cool. I splashed it with cologne and gave it a credit card for clout....

Then I opened the door, expecting to see a clean inside, but what I saw was putrid—a stinky and repulsive interior.

I could think of only one other option. My freezer needed some high-voltage pleasure! I immediately bought it some copies of *Playfridge* magazines—the publication that displays freezers with their doors open. I rented some films about foxy appliances.... I even tried to get my freezer a date with the Westinghouse next door, but she gave him the cold shoulder.

After a few days of supercharged, after-hours entertainment, I opened the door. And I nearly got sick.

I know what you're thinking. The only thing worse than Max's humor is his common sense. Who would concentrate on the outside when the problem is on the inside?

Do you really want to know?

A homemaker battles with depression. What is the solution suggested by some well-meaning friend? Buy a new dress.

A husband is involved in an affair that brings him as much guilt as it does adventure. The solution? Change peer groups. Hang out with people who don't make you feel guilty!

A young professional is plagued with loneliness. His obsession with success has left him with no friends. His boss gives him an idea: Change your style. Get a new haircut. Flash some cash.

Case after case of treating the outside while ignoring the inside—polishing the case while ignoring the interior. And what is the result?

The homemaker gets a new dress, and the depression disappears . . . for a day, maybe. Then the shadow returns.

The husband finds a bunch of buddies who sanction his adultery. The result? Peace . . . until the crowd is gone. Then the guilt is back.

The young professional gets a new look and the people notice . . . until the styles change. Then he has to scurry out and buy more stuff so he won't appear outdated.

The exterior polished; the interior corroding. The outside altered; the inside faltering. One thing is clear: Cosmetic changes are only skin deep.

By now you could write the message of the beatitude. It's a clear one: You change your life by changing your heart.

(from *The Applause of Heaven*
by Max Lucado)

RESPONSE

Use these questions to share more deeply with each other.

7. What traditions do you follow that are part of your religious heritage?

_____

_____

_____

8. What do you do in order to appear holy?

_____

_____

_____

9. When are you most likely to uphold outward religious tradition rather than honor God in your heart?

_____

_____

_____

PRAYER

Father, thank you for setting us free. We are no longer bound by the law, but saved through your grace. Keep us free from our own legalism, our own systems. Keep us amazed and mesmerized by what you have done for us.

JOURNALING

Take a few moments to record your personal insights from this lesson.

In what ways do I work harder to maintain an outward appearance of holiness rather than an inner holiness?

ADDITIONAL QUESTIONS

10. What is wrong with measuring spirituality by outward actions?

_____

_____

_____

11. How can you make sure traditions and outward actions do not replace true holiness?

_____

_____

_____

12. What can you do to ensure that you are clean in God's sight?

_____

_____

_____

For more Bible passages about having a pure heart, see Psalm 51; 94:8–11; Proverbs 4:23; 2 Corinthians 4:16–18; Hebrews 12:14.

To complete the book of Mark during this twelve-part study, read Mark 7:1–37.

ADDITIONAL THOUGHTS

LESSON EIGHT

TRUE DISCIPLESHIP

REFLECTION

Begin your study by sharing thoughts on this question.

1. Think of a time when your involvement in an activity required significant sacrifices. What aspects of your life did this affect?

_____

_____

_____

BIBLE READING

Read Mark 8:34–38 from the NCV or the NKJV.

NCV

34Then Jesus called the crowd to him, along with his followers. He said, "If people want to follow me, they must give up the things they want. They must be willing even to give up their lives to follow me. 35Those who want to save their lives will give up true life. But those who give up their lives for me and for the Good News will have true life. 36It is worth nothing for them to have the whole world if they lose their

NKJV

34When He had called the people to Himself, with His disciples also, He said to them, "Whoever desires to come after Me, let him deny himself, and take up his cross, and follow Me. 35For whoever desires to save his life will lose it, but whoever loses his life for My sake and the gospel's will save it. 36For what will it profit a man if he gains the whole world, and loses his own soul? 37Or what will a man give

NCV	NKJV
souls. ³⁷They could never pay enough to buy back their souls. ³⁸The people who live now are living in a sinful and evil time. If people are ashamed of me and my teaching, the Son of Man will be ashamed of them when he comes with his Father's glory and with the holy angels."	in exchange for his soul. ³⁸For whoever is ashamed of Me and My words in this adulterous and sinful generation, of him the Son of Man also will be ashamed when He comes in the glory of His Father with the holy angels."

DISCOVERY

Explore the Bible reading by discussing these questions.

2. What is the cost of true discipleship?

_____

_____

_____

3. How do some people react when they learn that being a true follower of Jesus is costly?

_____

_____

_____

4. What is your reaction to the cost of true discipleship?

_____

_____

_____

5. What does it mean to lose your life for Christ's sake?

_____

_____

_____

6. What does it mean to gain the whole world?

_____

_____

_____

INSPIRATION

Here is an uplifting thought from the *Inspirational Study Bible*.

The pole of power is greasy.

The Roman emperor Charlemagne knew that. An interesting story surrounds the burial of this famous king. Legend has it that he asked to be entombed sitting upright in his throne. He asked that his crown be placed on his head and his scepter in his hand. He requested that the royal cape be draped around his shoulders and an open book be placed in his lap.

That was A.D. 814. Nearly two hundred years later, Emperor Othello determined to see if the burial request had been carried out. He allegedly sent a team of men to open the tomb and make a report. They found the body just as Charlemagne had requested. Only now, nearly two centuries later, the scene was gruesome. The crown was tilted, the mantle moth-eaten, the body disfigured. But open on the skeletal thighs was the book Charlemagne had requested—the Bible. One bony finger pointed to Matthew 16:26: "What good will it be for a man if he gains the whole world, yet forfeits his soul?"

You can answer that one.

(from *The Applause of Heaven*
by Max Lucado)

RESPONSE

Use these questions to share more deeply with each other.

7. How are you trying to deny yourself and take up your cross?

_____

_____

_____

8. Think of a time when you wanted to hide the fact that you are a Christian. What made you want to keep quiet?

_____

_____

_____

9. How should a Christian's life be different from a non-Christian's life?

_____

_____

_____

PRAYER

Father, you have given us such a great promise, the promise of salvation. Forgive us when we sometimes put more hope in the things of this earth than in the incredible promises of your heaven.

JOURNALING

Take a few moments to record your personal insights from this lesson.

In what ways am I living for myself rather than for Christ?

ADDITIONAL QUESTIONS

10. What do you need to change to be a true disciple?

_____

_____

_____

11. What is the reward for the person who follows the commands given by Jesus?

_____

_____

_____

12. What is the difference between denying self and self-denial?

_____

_____

_____

For more Bible passages about living for God, see Matthew 4:18–21; 5:14–16; Luke 12:13–21; 12:29–33; John 12:25, 26; 13:5–17.

To complete the book of Mark during this twelve-part study, read Mark 8:1–38.

ADDITIONAL THOUGHTS

LESSON NINE

FAITH TO OVERCOME

REFLECTION

Begin your study by sharing thoughts on this question.

1. Think of a time when you didn't fully trust someone to do something. Why did you lack faith in that person?

_____

_____

_____

BIBLE READING

Read Mark 9:14–29 from the NCV or the NKJV.

NCV

¹⁴When Jesus, Peter, James, and John came back to the other followers, they saw a great crowd around them and the teachers of the law arguing with them. ¹⁵But as soon as the crowd saw Jesus, the people were surprised and ran to welcome him.

¹⁶Jesus asked, "What are you arguing about?"

NKJV

¹⁴And when He came to the disciples, He saw a great multitude around them, and scribes disputing with them. ¹⁵Immediately, when they saw Him, all the people were greatly amazed, and running to Him, greeted Him. ¹⁶And He asked the scribes, "What are you discussing with them?"

¹⁷Then one of the crowd answered and said,

NCV

¹⁷A man answered, "Teacher, I brought my son to you. He has an evil spirit in him that stops him from talking. ¹⁸When the spirit attacks him, it throws him on the ground. Then my son foams at the mouth, grinds his teeth, and becomes very stiff. I asked your followers to force the evil spirit out, but they couldn't."

¹⁹Jesus answered, "You people have no faith. How long must I stay with you? How long must I put up with you? Bring the boy to me."

²⁰So the followers brought him to Jesus. As soon as the evil spirit saw Jesus, it made the boy lose control of himself, and he fell down and rolled on the ground, foaming at the mouth.

²¹Jesus asked the boy's father, "How long has this been happening?"

The father answered, "Since he was very young. ²²The spirit often throws him into a fire or into water to kill him. If you can do anything for him, please have pity on us and help us."

²³Jesus said to the father, "You said, 'If you can!' All things are possible for the one who believes."

²⁴Immediately the father cried out, "I do believe! Help me to believe more!"

²⁵When Jesus saw that a crowd was quickly gathering, he ordered the evil spirit, saying, "You spirit that makes people unable to hear or speak, I command you to come out of this boy and never enter him again!"

²⁶The evil spirit screamed and caused the boy to fall on the ground again. Then the spirit came out. The boy looked as if he were dead, and many people said, "He is dead!" ²⁷But Jesus took hold of the boy's hand and helped him to stand up.

NKJV

"Teacher, I brought You my son, who has a mute spirit. ¹⁸And wherever it seizes him, it throws him down; he foams at the mouth, gnashes his teeth, and becomes rigid. So I spoke to Your disciples, that they should cast it out, but they could not."

¹⁹He answered him and said, "O faithless generation, how long shall I be with you? How long shall I bear with you? Bring him to Me." ²⁰Then they brought him to Him. And when he saw Him, immediately the spirit convulsed him, and he fell on the ground and wallowed, foaming at the mouth.

²¹So He asked his father, "How long has this been happening to him?"

And he said, "From childhood. ²²And often he has thrown him both into the fire and into the water to destroy him. But if You can do anything, have compassion on us and help us."

²³Jesus said to him, "If you can believe, all things are possible to him who believes."

²⁴Immediately the father of the child cried out and said with tears, "Lord, I believe; help my unbelief!"

²⁵When Jesus saw that the people came running together, He rebuked the unclean spirit, saying to it, "Deaf and dumb spirit, I command you, come out of him and enter him no more!" ²⁶Then the spirit cried out, convulsed him greatly, and came out of him. And he became as one dead, so that many said, "He is dead." ²⁷But Jesus took him by the hand and lifted him up, and he arose.

²⁸And when He had come into the house, His disciples asked Him privately, "Why could we not cast it out?"

NCV

²⁸When Jesus went into the house, his followers began asking him privately, "Why couldn't we force that evil spirit out?"

²⁹Jesus answered, "That kind of spirit can only be forced out by prayer."

NKJV

²⁹So He said to them, "This kind can come out by nothing but prayer and fasting."

DISCOVERY

Explore the Bible reading by discussing these questions.

2. What is Jesus' authority over other spirits?

_____

_____

_____

3. How do you think the father in this story felt after many years of caring for his son?

_____

_____

_____

4. How great was the faith of the father?

_____

_____

_____

5. Why were the disciples unable to heal the boy?

_____

_____

_____

6. Which character of this story can you identify with?

_____

_____

_____

INSPIRATION

Here is an uplifting thought from the *Inspirational Study Bible.*

Some of you pray like a Concorde jet—smooth, sleek, high, and mighty. Your words reverberate in the clouds and send sonic booms throughout the heavens. If you pray like a Concorde, I salute you. If you don't, I understand.

Maybe you are like me, more a crop duster than a Concorde. You aren't flashy, you fly low, you seem to cover the same ground a lot, and some mornings it's tough to get the old engine cranked up.

Most of us are like that. Most of our prayer lives could use a tune-up.

Some prayer lives lack consistency. They're either a desert or an oasis. Long, arid, dry spells interrupted by brief plunges into the waters of communion. We go days or weeks without consistent prayer, but then something happens—we hear a sermon, read a book, experience a tragedy—something leads us to pray, so we dive in. We submerge ourselves in prayer and leave refreshed and renewed. But as the journey resumes, our prayers don't.

Others of us need sincerity. Our prayers are a bit hollow, memorized, and rigid. More liturgy than life. And though they are daily, they are dull.

Still others lack, well, honesty. We honestly wonder if prayer makes a difference. Why on earth would God in heaven want to talk to me? If God knows all, who am I to tell him anything? If God controls all, who am I to do anything?

If you struggle with prayer, I've got just the guy for you. Don't worry, he's not a monastic saint. He's not a calloused-kneed apostle. Nor is he a prophet whose middle name is meditation. He's not a too-holy-to-be-you reminder of how far you need to go in prayer. He's just the opposite. A fellow crop duster. A parent with a sick son in need of a miracle. The father's prayer isn't much, but the answer is, and the result reminds us: The power is not in the prayer; it's in the one who hears it.

He prayed out of desperation. His son, his only son, was demon-possessed. Not only was he a deaf mute and an epileptic, he was also possessed by an evil spirit. Ever since the boy was young, the demon had thrown him into fires and water.

Imagine the pain of the father. Other dads could watch their children grow and mature; he could only watch his suffer. While others were teaching their sons an occupation, he was just trying to keep his son alive.

What a challenge! He couldn't leave his son alone for a minute. Who knew when the next attack would come? The father had to remain on call, on alert twenty-four hours a day. He was desperate and tired, and his prayer reflects both.

"If you can do anything for him, please have pity on us and help us."

Listen to that prayer. Does it sound courageous? Confident? Strong? Hardly.

One word would have made a lot of difference. Instead of *if*, what if he'd said *since*? "Since you can do anything for him, please have pity on us and help us."

But that's not what he said. He said *if.* The Greek is even more emphatic. The tense implies doubt. It's as if the man were saying, "This one's probably out of your league, but if you can ..."

A classic crop-duster appeal. More meek than might. More timid than towering. More like a crippled lamb coming to a shepherd than a proud lion roaring in the jungle. If his prayer sounds like yours, then don't be discouraged, for that's where prayer begins.

It begins as a yearning. An honest appeal. Ordinary people staring at Mount Everest. No pretense. No boasting. No posturing. Just prayer. Feeble prayer, but prayer nonetheless.

(from *He Still Moves Stones*
by Max Lucado)

RESPONSE

Use these questions to share more deeply with each other.

7. What kind of faith does Jesus require of us?

_____

_____

_____

8. When has your faith been challenged?

_____

_____

_____

9. How have these challenges helped to deepen your faith in God?

_____

_____

_____

PRAYER

Father, we cherish your promises to take care of your children. And yet we often come to you with muddled ideas, unsure of what is best, uncertain of your will. Thank you, Father, for the assurance that our imperfect prayers cannot hinder your incredible power.

JOURNALING

Take a few moments to record your personal insights from this lesson.

What are some promises from Scripture that I can memorize to strengthen my faith?

ADDITIONAL QUESTIONS

10. How does Jesus' promise, "If you can believe, all things are possible to him who believes," strengthen your faith?

_____

_____

_____

11. In what ways does the father's plea, "Lord, I believe; help my unbelief!" resonate with your prayers?

_____

_____

_____

12. How can you encourage others who are lacking faith?

_____

_____

_____

For more Bible passages about trusting God, see Genesis 18:1–14; Matthew 8:5–13; 9:27–31; Luke 11:9, 10; 12:22–34.

To complete the book of Mark during this twelve-part study, read Mark 9:1–50.

LESSON TEN

SALVATION THROUGH FAITH

REFLECTION

Begin your study by sharing thoughts on this question.

1. If you received an extraordinary amount of wealth, how would you spend it?

_____

_____

_____

BIBLE READING

Read Mark 10:17–31 from the NCV or the NKJV.

NCV

¹⁷As Jesus started to leave, a man ran to him and fell on his knees before Jesus. The man asked, "Good teacher, what must I do to have life forever?"

¹⁸Jesus answered, "Why do you call me good? Only God is good. ¹⁹You know the commands: 'You must not murder anyone. You must not be guilty of adultery. You must not steal. You

NKJV

¹⁷Now as He was going out on the road, one came running, knelt before Him, and asked Him, "Good Teacher, what shall I do that I may inherit eternal life?"

¹⁸So Jesus said to him, "Why do you call Me good? No one is good but One, that is, God. ¹⁹You know the commandments: 'Do not commit adultery,' 'Do not murder,' 'Do not steal,' 'Do

NCV

must not tell lies about your neighbor. You must not cheat. Honor your father and mother.'"

²⁰The man said, "Teacher, I have obeyed all these things since I was a boy."

²¹Jesus, looking at the man, loved him and said, "There is one more thing you need to do. Go and sell everything you have, and give the money to the poor, and you will have treasure in heaven. Then come and follow me."

²²He was very sad to hear Jesus say this, and he left sorrowfully, because he was rich.

²³Then Jesus looked at his followers and said, "How hard it will be for the rich to enter the kingdom of God!"

²⁴The followers were amazed at what Jesus said. But he said again, "My children, it is very hard to enter the kingdom of God! ²⁵It is easier for a camel to go through the eye of a needle than for a rich person to enter the kingdom of God."

²⁶The followers were even more surprised and said to each other, "Then who can be saved?"

²⁷Jesus looked at them and said, "This is something people cannot do, but God can. God can do all things."

²⁸Peter said to Jesus, "Look, we have left everything and followed you."

²⁹Jesus said, "I tell you the truth, all those who have left houses, brothers, sisters, mother, father, children, or farms for me and for the Good News ³⁰will get more than they left. Here in this world they will have a hundred times more homes, brothers, sisters, mothers, children, and fields. And with those things, they will also suffer for their belief. But in the age

NKJV

not bear false witness,' 'Do not defraud,' 'Honor your father and your mother.'"

²⁰And he answered and said to Him, "Teacher, all these things I have kept from my youth."

²¹Then Jesus, looking at him, loved him, and said to him, "One thing you lack: Go your way, sell whatever you have and give to the poor, and you will have treasure in heaven; and come, take up the cross, and follow Me."

²²But he was sad at this word, and went away sorrowful, for he had great possessions.

²³Then Jesus looked around and said to His disciples, "How hard it is for those who have riches to enter the kingdom of God!" ²⁴And the disciples were astonished at His words. But Jesus answered again and said to them, "Children, how hard it is for those who trust in riches to enter the kingdom of God! ²⁵It is easier for a camel to go through the eye of a needle than for a rich man to enter the kingdom of God."

²⁶And they were greatly astonished, saying among themselves, "Who then can be saved?"

²⁷But Jesus looked at them and said, "With men it is impossible, but not with God; for with God all things are possible."

²⁸Then Peter began to say to Him, "See, we have left all and followed You."

²⁹So Jesus answered and said, "Assuredly, I say to you, there is no one who has left house or brothers or sisters or father or mother or wife or children or lands, for My sake and the gospel's, ³⁰who shall not receive a hundredfold now in this time—houses and brothers and sisters and mothers and children and lands, with persecutions—and in the age to come,

NCV

that is coming they will have life forever. ³¹Many who have the highest place now will have the lowest place in the future. And many who have the lowest place now will have the highest place in the future."

NKJV

eternal life. ³¹But many who are first will be last, and the last first."

DISCOVERY

Explore the Bible reading by discussing these questions.

2. Why did the young man think he would inherit eternal life?

_____

_____

_____

3. Why couldn't the young man accept Jesus' requirements for eternal life?

_____

_____

_____

4. Why is it difficult for the rich to enter the kingdom of God?

_____

_____

_____

5. What was Jesus trying to teach his disciples about eternal life?

_____

_____

_____

6. What does Peter's response to Jesus reveal about his attitude toward eternal life?

_____

_____

_____

INSPIRATION

Here is an uplifting thought from the *Inspirational Study Bible*.

Jesus gets to the point. "If you want to be perfect, then go sell your possessions and give to the poor, and you will have treasure in heaven."

The statement leaves the young man distraught and the disciples bewildered.

Their question could be ours: "Who then can be saved?"

Jesus' answer shell-shocks the listeners, "With man this is impossible. . . ."

Impossible.

He doesn't say improbable. He doesn't say unlikely. He doesn't even say it will be tough. He says it is "impossible.". . .

Does that strike you as cold? All your life

you've been rewarded according to your performance. You get grades according to your study. You get commendations according to your success. You get money in response to your work.

That's why the rich young ruler thought heaven was just a payment away. It only made sense. You work hard, you pay your dues, and "zap"—your account is credited as paid in full. Jesus says, "No way." What you want costs far more than what you can pay. You don't need a system, you need a Savior. You don't need a resume, you need a Redeemer. For "what is impossible with men is possible with God."

…You see, it wasn't the money that hindered the rich man; it was the self-sufficiency. It wasn't the possessions; it was the pomp. It wasn't the big bucks; it was the big head.…

Astounding. These people are standing before the throne of God and bragging about themselves. The great trumpet has sounded, and they are still tooting their own horns. Rather than sing his praises, they sing their own. Rather than worship God, they read their resumes. When they should be speechless, they speak. In the very aura of the King they boast of self. What is worse—their arrogance or their blindness?

…God does not save us because of what we've done.…

And only a great God does for his children what they can't do for themselves.

That is the message of Paul: "For what the law was powerless to do…God did."

And that is the message of the first beatitude.

"Blessed are the poor in spirit…"

The jewel of joy is given to the impoverished spirits, not the affluent. God's delight is received upon surrender, not awarded upon conquest.

(from *The Applause of Heaven*
by Max Lucado)

RESPONSE

Use these questions to share more deeply with each other.

7. In what ways are you measuring obedience to God by external actions rather than internal attitudes?

_____

_____

_____

8. Why can we get so easily distracted by riches?

_____

_____

_____

9. What does it mean that the first will be last and the last will be first?

_____

_____

_____

PRAYER

Father, keep us from being so blinded by possessions we cannot keep that we fail to see the eternal treasure we cannot lose.

JOURNALING

Take a few moments to record your personal insights from this lesson.

How can I avoid the trap of putting my confidence in things rather than in God?

ADDITIONAL QUESTIONS

10. What should be the attitude of believers toward wealth?

_____

_____

_____

11. What is Jesus' promise to those who give up treasures of this world for his sake and the gospel's?

_____

_____

_____

12. What, in addition to money, can distract people who want to follow God?

_____

_____

_____

For more Bible passages about the deceitfulness of riches, see Proverbs 28:11; 28:20; Matthew 15:21–28; Mark 8:36, 37; Luke 12:15–21; 16:19–31.

To complete the book of Mark during this twelve-part study, read Mark 10:1–52.

LESSON ELEVEN

THE GREATEST COMMANDMENT

REFLECTION

Begin your study by sharing thoughts on this question.

1. Think of someone you love very much. How do you show that person your love?

_____

_____

_____

BIBLE READING

Read Mark 12:28–34 from the NCV or the NKJV.

NCV

28One of the teachers of the law came and heard Jesus arguing with the Sadducees. Seeing that Jesus gave good answers to their questions, he asked Jesus, "Which of the commands is most important?"

29Jesus answered, "The most important command is this: 'Listen, people of Israel! The Lord our God is the only Lord. 30Love the Lord your God with all your heart, all your soul, all your mind, and all your strength.' 31The second

NKJV

28Then one of the scribes came, and having heard them reasoning together, perceiving that He had answered them well, asked Him, "Which is the first commandment of all?"

29Jesus answered him, "The first of all the commandments is: 'Hear, O Israel, the LORD our God, the LORD is one. 30And you shall love the LORD your God with all your heart, with all your soul, with all your mind, and with all your strength.' This is the first commandment. 31And

NCV

command is this: 'Love your neighbor as you love yourself.' There are no commands more important than these."

³²The man answered, "That was a good answer, Teacher. You were right when you said God is the only Lord and there is no other God besides him. ³³One must love God with all his heart, all his mind, and all his strength. And one must love his neighbor as he loves himself. These commands are more important than all the animals and sacrifices we offer to God."

³⁴When Jesus saw that the man answered him wisely, Jesus said to him, "You are close to the kingdom of God." And after that, no one was brave enough to ask Jesus any more questions.

NKJV

the second, like it, is this: 'You shall love your neighbor as yourself.' There is no other commandment greater than these."

³²So the scribe said to Him, "Well said, Teacher. You have spoken the truth, for there is one God, and there is no other but He. ³³And to love Him with all the heart, with all the understanding, with all the soul, and with all the strength, and to love one's neighbor as oneself, is more than all the whole burnt offerings and sacrifices."

³⁴Now when Jesus saw that he answered wisely, He said to him, "You are not far from the kingdom of God."

But after that no one dared question Him.

DISCOVERY

Explore the Bible reading by discussing these questions.

2. What kind of love are we commanded to have for God?

_____

_____

_____

3. What does it mean to love God with all your heart, soul, mind, and strength?

_____

_____

_____

4. How do you love yourself?

_____

_____

_____

5. Think of a time when you witnessed a loving deed. What impressed you most about the situation?

_____

_____

_____

6. What did Jesus say is the most important thing in life?

_____

_____

_____

INSPIRATION

Here is an uplifting thought from the *Inspirational Study Bible*.

Love for the Master is not some sweet sentimental emotion that sweeps over the soul in moments of special piety. Love for Christ is a deliberate setting of the will to carry out His commands at any cost. It is the fixed attitude of heart that decides to do His will at all times. It is the desire and delight of accomplishing our Father's highest purposes, no matter how challenging.

The end result of such conduct for a Christian is to bring sweet satisfaction to the great Good Shepherd of his soul. Because of such bold and single-minded service we sense His approval of our behavior. We sense and know of a surety that we are loved and appreciated. We are His friends. And the ultimate end is that others benefit; others are blessed; others are cared for....

In our highly permissive society, where the so-called "me" generation is encouraged to be so self-centered and so self-preoccupied, the call to obey Christ and comply with His commands cuts across our culture and our cynical conduct.

It simply is not normal nor natural for most of us to "love" God or "love" others in the drastic discipline of a laid-down life. We are a selfish, self-serving people. And when called upon to serve others we feel insulted. We have the strange, worldly idea that to be of lowly service is to be "used" or "abused."

Yet God, very God, in Christ came among us in lowly service. He came to minister to us. He came to give Himself to us. And so, because He first "loved" us, we in turn are to be willing and ready to "love" Him and others.

(from *Lessons from a Sheep Dog* by Phillip Keller)

RESPONSE

Use these questions to share more deeply with each other.

7. In which aspect—your heart, soul, or mind—do you find it most difficult to love God? Why?

_____

_____

_____

8. Why is it challenging to love God as he commands?

_____

_____

_____

9. Why do we struggle to love our neighbors as ourselves?

_____

_____

_____

PRAYER

God, give us strength as we try to be more like Jesus in our lives. We ask you to keep the evil one away from us; keep us close to you, Father. Let our lives be testimonies of your love for us, that when people see our lives, they would see how you have loved the world.

JOURNALING

Take a few moments to record your personal insights from this lesson.

How can I show others a more sacrificial love?

ADDITIONAL QUESTIONS

10. How are the two commandments interrelated?

_____

_____

_____

11. What does it mean when a person is not far from the kingdom of God?

_____

_____

_____

12. In what ways is the command to love God different from the human emotion of love?

_____

_____

_____

For more Bible passages about loving God and others, see Matthew 5:43, 44; John 13:34; Romans 12:9; 1 Corinthians 13:4–8; Ephesians 5:2; 1 John 4:7–12, 19–21; 5:1–3; 2 John 5.

To complete the book of Mark during this twelve-part study, read Mark 11:1–13:37.

ADDITIONAL THOUGHTS

LESSON TWELVE

ADORATION

REFLECTION

Begin your study by sharing thoughts on this question.

1. Think of the most meaningful gift you have ever given to someone. How did that person respond to your gift?

_____

_____

_____

BIBLE READING

Read Mark 14:3–9 from the NCV or the NKJV.

NCV

³Jesus was in Bethany at the house of Simon, who had a skin disease. While Jesus was eating there, a woman approached him with an alabaster jar filled with very expensive perfume, made of pure nard. She opened the jar and poured the perfume on Jesus' head.

⁴Some who were there became upset and said to each other, "Why waste that perfume?

NKJV

³And being in Bethany at the house of Simon the leper, as He sat at the table, a woman came having an alabaster flask of very costly oil of spikenard. Then she broke the flask and poured it on His head. ⁴But there were some who were indignant among themselves, and said, "Why was this fragrant oil wasted? ⁵For it might have been sold for more than three

NCV

⁵It was worth a full year's work. It could have been sold and the money given to the poor." And they got very angry with the woman.

⁶Jesus said, "Leave her alone. Why are you troubling her? She did an excellent thing for me. ⁷You will always have the poor with you, and you can help them anytime you want. But you will not always have me. ⁸This woman did the only thing she could do for me; she poured perfume on my body to prepare me for burial. ⁹I tell you the truth, wherever the Good News is preached in all the world, what this woman has done will be told, and people will remember her."

NKJV

hundred denarii and given to the poor." And they criticized her sharply.

⁶But Jesus said, "Let her alone. Why do you trouble her? She has done a good work for Me. ⁷For you have the poor with you always, and whenever you wish you may do them good; but Me you do not have always. ⁸She has done what she could. She has come beforehand to anoint My body for burial. ⁹Assuredly, I say to you, wherever this gospel is preached in the whole world, what this woman has done will also be told as a memorial to her."

DISCOVERY

Explore the Bible reading by discussing these questions.

2. Why was the woman criticized for her actions?

_____

_____

_____

3. How might the woman have felt after Jesus affirmed her actions?

_____

_____

_____

4. Why did the woman choose to anoint Jesus at that time?

_____

_____

_____

5. What was the significance of the woman's actions?

_____

_____

_____

6. Picture yourself in the room with Jesus, the disciples, and the woman. How would you have responded to this very expensive gift?

_____

_____

_____

INSPIRATION

Here is an uplifting thought from the *Inspirational Study Bible*.

"The people," Matthew wrote, "were amazed when they saw the mute speaking, the crippled made well, the lame walking, and the blind seeing."

...Then Matthew, still the great economizer of words, gave us another phrase on which I wish he would have elaborated:

"They praised the God of Israel."

I wonder how they did that? I feel more certain of what they *didn't* do than of what they did do. I feel confident that they didn't form a praise committee. I feel confident that they didn't make any robes. I feel confident that they didn't sit in rows and stare at the back of each other's heads.

I doubt seriously if they wrote a creed on how they were to praise this God they had never before worshiped. I can't picture them getting into an argument over technicalities. I doubt if they felt it had to be done indoors.

And I know they didn't wait until the Sabbath to do it....

I can imagine throngs of people pushing and shoving. Wanting to get close. Not to request anything or demand anything, but just to say "thank you."

...However they did it, they did it. And Jesus was touched, so touched that he insisted they stay for a meal before they left....

Worship is the "thank you" that refuses to be silenced.

We have tried to make a science out of worship. We can't do that. We can't do that any more than we can "sell love" or "negotiate peace."

Worship is a voluntary act of gratitude offered by the saved to the Savior, by the healed to the Healer, and by the delivered to the Deliverer.

(from *In the Eye of the Storm*
by Max Lucado)

RESPONSE

Use these questions to share more deeply with each other.

7. Have you ever been criticized for loving God? In what ways?

_____

_____

_____

8. How should you respond to those who criticize your love for God?

_____

_____

_____

9. What are you willing to sacrifice to worship God?

_____

_____

_____

PRAYER

Father, help us to maintain our promise of faithfulness to you, even in times when we are surrounded by people who oppose your kingdom. Give us great courage as we face the challenges of following you.

JOURNALING

Take a few moments to record your personal insights from this lesson.

How does this story inspire me to pour out my heart in worship?

ADDITIONAL QUESTIONS

10. In what ways does the example of this woman challenge your view of worship?

_____

_____

_____

11. Why was it difficult for the others to see the value in what the woman did for Jesus?

_____

_____

_____

12. Why do you think the woman in the story chose to offer this gift to Jesus?

_____

_____

_____

For more Bible passages about adoring God, see Exodus 3:1–6; 34:14; Psalm 29:12; Luke 10:38–42; Hebrews 12:28; James 4:8.

To complete the book of Mark during this twelve-part study, read Mark 14:1–16:20.

ADDITIONAL THOUGHTS

ADDITIONAL THOUGHTS

_____

_____

_____

_____

_____

_____

_____

_____

_____

_____

_____

_____

_____

_____

_____

_____

_____

_____

_____

_____

_____

ADDITIONAL THOUGHTS

LEADERS' NOTES

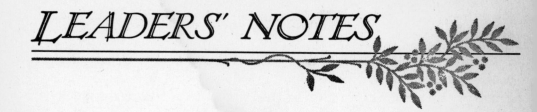

LESSON ONE

Question 1: Be prepared to share your answer first, since some group members might be uncomfortable describing a time when they were hurting.

Question 2: The leper believed Jesus was *able* to heal him, but he was not sure whether Jesus was *willing* to heal him because lepers were outcasts.

Question 3: Jesus understood the loneliness and isolation the leper had experienced. Undoubtedly, Jesus' loving touch was the first this man had felt in a long time.

Question 5: Imagine being healed from a life threatening disease and then being asked not to say anything about it. How would you respond?

LESSON TWO

Question 2: The men risked their lives and the paralytic's life since the roof was weakened from the hole they were making.

Question 3: The scribes knew that only God can forgive sins. They rightly interpreted Jesus' claim to forgive sins as a claim to be God.

Question 4: The physical healing proved Jesus had the power to forgive sins.

LESSON THREE

Question 2: The types of soil represent the different ways we might respond to the Word of God: The wayside is the hard heart that resists the Word of God. Just like hard ground must be plowed before it can receive the seed, hearts must be softened before they can receive the Word. The stony ground is the shallow heart. Since there is no depth to the soil, wherever a seed falls it will not take root. People who are like the stony ground hear the Word and get excited for a short time, but when trials come, they turn away from God. The thorny soil represents the crowded heart. These people hear the Word of God, but they are too involved with the cares of their lives to make changes. The issues of life crowd out the Word and hinder growth. The good ground is the fruitful heart. The lives of people whose hearts are good soil give evidence of true salvation.

Question 4: You could ask the group these additional questions: Are you the stony ground and having trouble committing to the price of Christianity? Are you the thorny soil where there is so much activity that you do not have time to listen to God or respond to what He is saying? Are you the good ground bearing fruit?

Question 8: Point out that Satan is very subtle in his ways. Some possibilities include self-centeredness, fatigue, pride, self-reliance, bitterness, busyness, and unforgiveness.

LESSON FOUR

Question 3: Even though the disciples had spent quality time with Jesus, heard him speak, and witnessed his miracles, they were still doubtful about his identity and did not fully trust him. They lacked faith in his ability to handle any situation.

Question 12: Consider sharing how you have been encouraged during a troubling time.

LESSON FIVE

Question 2: Jairus risked his reputation and livelihood in order to save his daughter's life. He was an important, wealthy synagogue leader, but most of the other synagogue leaders were opposed to Jesus.

Question 3: Because of the woman's bleeding disorder, she was ceremonially unclean. Everything she touched would be unclean. She was an outcast from society. To enter the crowd meant risking the possibility of touching someone or being recognized as an outcast.

Question 7: Some may find it difficult to identify with the bleeding woman. Be prepared to share your answer first.

LESSON SIX

Question 2: Scripture tells us Jesus stayed back to pray (verse 46), but we might wonder if he was also testing their faith. This incident is also recorded in Matthew 14:22–33.

Question 5: Consider asking the group this follow-up question: What prevents us from recognizing Jesus? Why?

LESSON SEVEN

Question 4: Jesus exposed the hypocrisy of the Pharisees. Their worship came not from their hearts but from their desire to appear holy. He accused them of teaching that their traditions were more important than God's commandments.

Question 6: The disciples had grown up with the strict Jewish dietary codes that categorized clean and unclean foods, so it was hard for them to alter their thinking and change religious traditions that they had been practicing for years.

Question 8: Include attitudes, words, and ministries as well as actions in your discussion.

LESSON EIGHT

Question 4: Reactions to the cost of discipleship change as Christians mature. Encourage group members to share their reactions at different times in their lives.

Question 5: If you lose your life for Christ's sake, your motivation is no longer living for yourself but for Christ and his ultimate purposes. In the world's eyes you are accomplishing nothing; you appear to be missing great opportunities.

Question 12: Self-denial is not the same as denying self. We practice self-denial when we give up things or activities that we want. God's will does not play a role in self-denial. However, when we deny self we surrender ourselves to Christ and determine to obey his will. As we mature in our faith, our own desires will be increasingly aligned with God's will.

LESSON NINE

Question 3: The father was probably tired, frustrated, and desperate. He had been dealing with this situation since his son was a child. It was painful for him to watch the effect the spirit had on his son; he was powerless to do anything to help. As a parent he might have been wishing he could take his son's place, since it is easier to experience pain personally rather than watch a loved one go through it.

Question 5: The authority Jesus had given them was effective only if exercised by faith. Perhaps the disciples lacked faith (verse 19) or failed to pray (verse 29).

LESSON TEN

Question 3: The man measured obedience by external actions rather than inward attitudes. He wanted salvation on his own terms and thus went away disappointed.

Question 4: If we possess money, we should be grateful and use it for God's glory, but we should not let money possess us. It is not bad to have the things that money can buy as long as we do not trade them for the things that money cannot buy.

Question 6: Peter's response indicates that his attitude was one of "giving to get." He felt that because he and his fellow disciples had given up something, they would certainly get something in return.

Question 8: Many people are distracted by attempts to become financially comfortable. Discuss why it is easy to get distracted by having "enough money."

LESSON ELEVEN

Question 3: Be sure to discuss practical examples.

Question 6: The Jews had cluttered their faith with rituals and rules they were obligated to obey. One of the favorite pasttimes of the leaders was to debate which law was the most important. All the laws, ceremonies, and rituals were placed in perspective when Jesus focused their attention on our central duty to love God and our neighbors.

Question 10: Be sure to note that we can never really know the state of another's heart.

LESSON TWELVE

Question 5: This woman gave her best in faith and love. Jesus said her actions would be remembered, and his prediction has come true. The account of her deed is recorded in three gospels, and her actions continue to be a blessing to the whole world.

Question 8: No matter what others say about our worship and service, the most important thing is that we please God. Our concern should be for his approval alone.

ADDITIONAL NOTES

ADDITIONAL NOTES

ADDITIONAL NOTES

ADDITIONAL NOTES

ACKNOWLEDGMENTS

Keller, Phillip. *Lessons from a Sheep Dog*, copyright 1983, Word, Inc., Dallas, Texas.

Lucado, Max. *The Applause of Heaven*, copyright 1990, Word, Inc., Dallas, Texas.

Lucado, Max. *He Still Moves Stones*, copyright 1993, Word, Inc., Dallas, Texas.

Lucado, Max. *In the Eye of the Storm*, copyright 1991, Word, Inc., Dallas, Texas.

Lucado, Max. *On the Anvil*, copyright 1985 by Max Lucado. Used by permission of Tyndale House Publishers, Inc. All rights reserved.

Lucado, Max. *Six Hours One Friday*, Questar Publishers, Multnomah Books, copyright 1989 by Max Lucado.

Smalley, Gary and John Trent. *The Gift of the Blessing*, copyright 1993 by Thomas Nelson, Nashville, Tennessee.